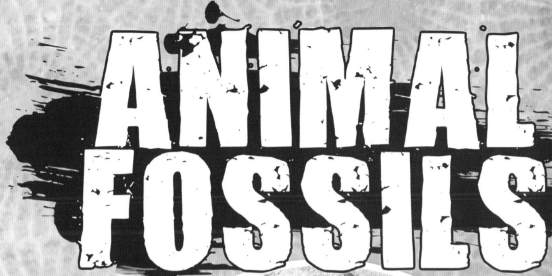

ANIMAL FOSSILS

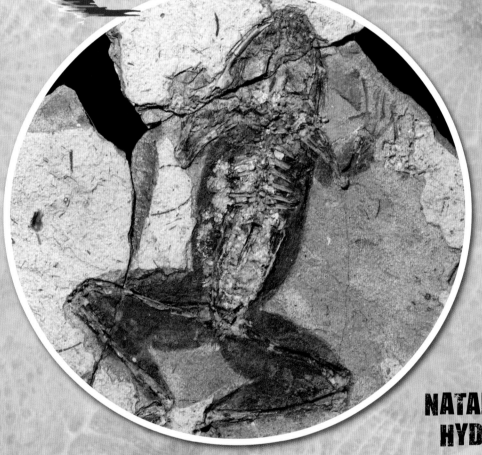

NATALIE HYDE

Crabtree Publishing Company

www.crabtreebooks.com

IF THESE FOSSILS COULD TALK

Author
Natalie Hyde

Publishing plan research and development
Reagan Miller

Editors
Adrianna Morganelli, Crystal Sikkens

Proofreader
Molly Aloian

Indexer
Wendy Scavuzzo

Design
Margaret Amy Salter

Photo research
Margaret Amy Salter, Crystal Sikkens

**Production coordinator
and prepress technician**
Samara Parent

Print coordinator
Margaret Amy Salter

Photographs
Alamy: © Stocktrek Images, Inc.: page 22 (middle)
Science Source: Sinclair Stammers: page 15 (top); Jane Burton /
  Warren Photographic: page 21 (top); Kjell B. Sandved:
  page 24
Thinkstock: cover (foreground), pages 3, 7 (top), 23 (bottom)
Wikimedia Commons: © Mauricio Antón: page 4; © Kevin
  Walsh: page 6 (top); © Sterilgutassistentin: page 11 (bottom);
  © Emőke Dénes: page 12; © Wilson44691: page 16 (left);
  © Smokeybjb: page 16 (right); © Nobu Tamura: page 17
  (top); © Smith609: page 17 (bottom); © Zina Deretsky:
  page 19 (top); © Scarlet23: page 19 (bottom);
  © User:Captmondo: page 20; © Mike Beauregard: page 21
  (bottom); © Ghedoghedo: page 22 (bottom); © H. Raab:
  page 25 (bottom); © Nobu Tamura: page 26 (top);
  © Ghedoghedo: page 26 (bottom); © Karthickbala:
  page 27 (bottom)
All other images by Shutterstock

Library and Archives Canada Cataloguing in Publication

Hyde, Natalie, 1963-, author
      Animal fossils / Natalie Hyde.

(If these fossils could talk)
Includes index.
Issued in print and electronic formats.
ISBN 978-0-7787-1261-9 (bound).--ISBN 978-0-7787-1265-7
(pbk.).--ISBN 978-1-4271-8955-4 (pdf).--ISBN 978-1-4271-8951-6
(html)

      1. Animals, Fossil--Juvenile literature. I. Title.

QE765.H93 2013   j560   C2013-905231-3
                                      C2013-905232-1

Mar 14 J

Library of Congress Cataloging-in-Publication Data

Hyde, Natalie, 1963-
  Animal fossils / Natalie Hyde.
      pages cm. -- (If these fossils could talk)
  Includes index.
  ISBN 978-0-7787-1261-9 (reinforced library binding : alk. paper) -- ISBN
978-0-7787-1265-7 (pbk. : alk. paper) -- ISBN (invalid) 978-1-4271-8955-4
(electronic pdf : alk. paper) -- ISBN 978-1-4271-8951-6 (electronic html :
alk. paper)
  1. Animals, Fossil--Juvenile literature. I. Title.

  QE765.H94 2014
  560--dc23
                                          2013033220

Crabtree Publishing Company

Printed in Canada/092013/BF20130815

www.crabtreebooks.com   1-800-387-7650

**Published in Canada
Crabtree Publishing**
616 Welland Ave.
St. Catharines, Ontario
L2M 5V6

**Published in the United States
Crabtree Publishing**
PMB 59051
350 Fifth Avenue, 59th Floor
New York, New York 10118

**Published in the United Kingdom
Crabtree Publishing**
Maritime House
Basin Road North, Hove
BN41 1WR

**Published in Australia
Crabtree Publishing**
3 Charles Street
Coburg North
VIC 3058

CONTENTS

Reliving the Past   4

Made in Many Ways   6

I'm Stuck!   8

A Sticky Situation   10

Nature's Freezer   12

Just a Trace   14

The Seafloor   16

Under the Sea   18

Slither and Crawl   20

Giant Mammals   22

Feathers and Flight   24

Past and Present   26

Fun with Fossils   28

Glossary   30

Learning More   31

Index   32

RELIVING THE PAST

When living things die, their remains usually rot away to nothing. But sometimes their bodies are quickly buried and trapped in the earth where they are preserved. These preserved remains are called fossils.

MYTHS OF MONSTERS

People have been collecting fossils since ancient times. Our **ancestors** used folktales and myths to explain the strange fossil bones and imprints they would find. The ancient Greeks found and displayed a huge bone of a woolly rhinoceros at the acropolis in the town of Nichoria. Researchers wonder if these bones played a part in inspiring the beasts of Greek myths. They find it interesting that ancient fossils are found in the same places where myths of giant creatures existed.

The ancient Greeks believed the huge bones they found were from human-like giants. Likely, these bones were from the giant woolly mammoths (left) or the woolly rhinoceroses (right).

FOSSIL EXPERTS

Paleontologists are scientists who study fossils. The animal fossil record can teach us important information about how animals **adapt** to different soil, climate, and temperatures. They also give us a look at the **diversity** of animal life on Earth from tiny insects and strange ocean sponges and jellyfish, to fierce reptiles and massive mammals. The fossil record shows how animals have changed and died off as Earth changed.

The earliest known animal fossils are 600 million years old. The fossilized bodies of blue-green algae, called Cyanobacteria, formed rock columns called stromatolites.

*Mammoths and mastodons are an **extinct** group of mammals related to elephants.*

NOTEWORTHY NAMES

Georges Cuvier is called the father of paleontology. He was the first to suggest that fossils belonged to animals that had become extinct. He was also the first to correctly identify large elephant-like bones as belonging to a mastodon.

MADE IN MANY WAYS

Animal fossils can form in different ways. Each process creates a different kind of fossil such as molds, casts, and mineralized or frozen fossils.

TURNED TO STONE

Mineralized fossils form when minerals seep into the hard parts of an animal's body such as teeth, bones, and shells. Over millions of years, these parts will turn to stone. Animals that are covered by **sediment** can leave an impression of their outside shape once they have **decomposed**. This is called a mold. Sometimes minerals collect inside the mold and harden. This creates a 3D model of the original animal. These fossils are called casts and can show amazing detail.

This cast shows a fossil of an early reptile.

Minerals turned these ammonite shells into rock.

LAYERS IN TIME

Animal fossils are often trapped in layers of rock. Paleontologists can "read" the fossil's history by digging down through the earth. They can find out which time period the animal lived in before becoming extinct. Some creatures only lived during a specific time in our Earth's history. Therefore, they are found only in one layer of rock. These fossils, called index fossils, are used as guides to date other fossils.

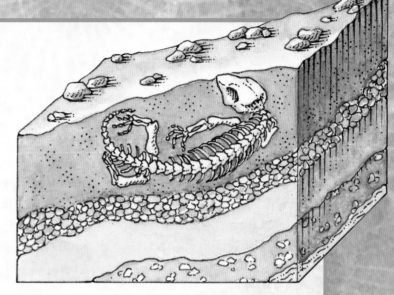

Animals that are found in rock layers near the surface lived in more recent time periods than animals found in lower layers.

PRESERVED FOREVER

Other materials, such as ice, can also preserve remains. **Glaciers** are huge rivers of ice. Sometimes creatures fall into cracks and are flash frozen, preserving not only bones and teeth, but also soft tissue such as flesh, hair, and fur. Tar pits and peat bogs do not contain the **bacteria** that eat away at remains. Animals trapped in these areas are preserved and do not decompose.

FACT FILE

Trilobites are an extinct type of marine animal. Paleontologists know that they lived from 521 million years ago until they died out about 250 million years ago. They are one of the best-known index fossils.

I'M STUCK!

Amber is fossilized tree resin. Resin is a sticky substance that oozes out of trees. As it oozed down the trunk or branch, small insects or bits of plants got stuck in it. Over time, the resin hardened into amber and the insect or plant material was preserved inside.

THE SMALLEST DETAILS

Amber is an important fossil because it can preserve soft or small parts that would normally decompose. Tiny hairs, feathers, bacteria, and even spider webs have been found in amber. Amber also captures a snapshot of a habitat. Leaves, pollen, or flowers found with insects can show the animal's food source or simply which plants existed at the same time.

scorpion preserved in amber

These insects were trapped in tree resin 40–50 million years ago.

WHAT WILL FIT?

The largest creatures found in amber are little gecko-like lizards. Birds are too large to be found in amber, but paleontologists have found a hummingbird egg. (They are about the size of a Tic Tac candy.)

ANCIENT AMBER

The oldest amber is approximately 320 million years old. Scientists are not sure what type of tree or plant produced it. Studies on the amber seem to suggest it is from a flowering plant, however, flowering plants had not yet evolved. The amber does not contain any animals or plant parts. Insects did not come along until many million years later. The oldest animals found in amber are two 230-million-year-old mites. Most amber fossils with insects, however, are no more than 150 million years old.

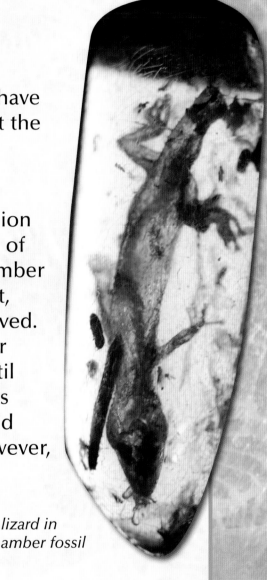

lizard in amber fossil

? How come animal fossils in casts or molds do not contain hair or feathers?

A STICKY SITUATION

Tar pits and peat bogs are natural formations where paleontologists have found preserved animal remains. A tar pit is a lake of asphalt instead of water. Tar pits are a gooey deathtrap that have preserved all types and sizes of creatures.

HIDDEN TRAP

The gooey surface of a tar pit was often covered with dirt, leaves, or water. This camouflage caused many different kinds of animals to step in the pit without knowing, becoming trapped. Some of the animals found in the La Brea Tar Pits in Los Angeles, California, are mammoths, dire wolves, sloths, bears, and even sabre-toothed cats. Fossilized insects and plants are also found in the tar and suggest the area had a cooler, wetter climate thousands of years ago.

Visitors can tour the La Brea Tar Pits, but all the pits are fenced off so tourists do not fall in and become fossils themselves!

GETTING BOGGED DOWN

Peat bogs form in wetlands. The bacteria that normally break down a dead body cannot live in the **acidic** water of bogs. Bodies that fall in a bog do not rot but often turn an orange color because of the chemicals.

NO WAY OUT

Once a creature became stuck in a peat bog, it was impossible for it to get out again. Most animals avoided these areas, but the bones of the Auroch, an ancestor to cows, can be found in the bogs of Northern Germany.

This peat bog is located in the Scottish highlands.

FACT FILE

Remains of a creature called the Irish Elk have been found in peat bogs across Europe. It was neither Irish nor an elk, but rather a prehistoric deer. This ancient creature stood over 7 feet (2 meters) tall and had antlers 12 feet (3.7 m) across.

NATURE'S FREEZER

Freezing temperatures can preserve animal bodies for thousands of years. Mountain rivers, freezing lakes, and glaciers are all places where animals can get trapped in an icy tomb.

FLASH FREEZE

Some animals became frozen fossils when they fell through thin ice over a lake, or were swept away in a flash flood. Others may have been crossing glaciers when they fell in a **crevasse**, or large crack. Mastodons, woolly mammoths, and giant camels are some of the wildlife caught in icy tombs.

NOW YOU SEE ME...

Freezing temperatures help to preserve all of the animal, not just the hard parts. This allows paleontologists to see what extinct animals really looked like. They can also measure the size of muscles, the thickness of the coat, and the amount of fur or hair.

Information found in mammoth hair gives scientists a good idea of the living conditions and climate in the past.

A REAL JURASSIC PARK?

Freezing can also preserve deoxyribonucleic acid (DNA). DNA is the blueprint information in each cell of a living thing. Scientists are trying to save and examine the DNA from frozen, extinct animals. Perhaps some day they can clone a woolly mammoth or a cave bear.

DNA

Mammoth and baby

Scientists have discovered a young woolly mammoth that contains a valuable piece of information. There are cut marks on its skin that look like they were made by a knife. This could be the first proof that early humans hunted and ate woolly mammoths.

ARCTIC ARTIFACT

Almost complete bodies of frozen woolly mammoths have been found in Siberia. Most are young mammoths that are still quite small—for a mammoth! Their small size might have helped to keep them covered with material to prevent them from rotting.

JUST A TRACE

Some fossils are not created from animal parts, but instead are evidence of their activity. Footprints, trails, nests, and even fossilized poop are all considered trace fossils. While normal fossils give information about the death of an organism, **trace fossils give us information about its life.**

STEP BY STEP

Fossil footprints give paleontologists a lot of information about the animal that made them. The deeper the print, the heavier the animal was. The distance between the left and right footprint will give clues to the width of their body. The location of footprints also point to changes in the environment. Most footprints were made in damp clay or dirt, so what was once a shoreline or swamp might now be a valley or field.

The pattern of footprints give clues to how animals moved.

FOSSILIZED *WHAT?*

Coprolites are fossilized animal dung. Animal droppings can help scientists understand the health and diet of the animal who left them. Seeds, pollen, or animal bones in the dung let paleontologists understand whether the animal was a herbivore (plant-eater) or carnivore (meat-eater). **Parasites** in the dung could indicate sickness.

The Reverend William Buckland from England was the first paleontologist to realize the importance of fossil poop, which he named "coprolite" or "dung-stone." The plant and animal remains in the dung gave him information about the animal's habitat.

(above) These coprolites are from ancient fish and turtles that lived 23 to 65 million years ago.

The oldest known dinosaur eggs are about 190 million years old.

PREHISTORIC PARENTS

Fossilized nests and eggs show what kind of parents these animals were. They can tell us whether the adults buried their eggs and left them to hatch on their own, or if nests were built above ground, where the parents sat on top of their eggs to provide warmth.

THE SEAFLOOR

The seafloor is a perfect place for fossilization. The oceans are constantly laying down layers of fine sediment. Creatures that die sink to the bottom and are quickly covered by layers of mud and silt.

CREATING A CAST

These layers build up, pressing the creature's tough **exterior** into the ground, leaving an image of its body. This image is called a mold fossil. Sometimes minerals fill the empty shape to create a cast, which is a 3D recreation of the shape of a long gone creature.

SEA LIFE IN BURGESS SHALE

The Burgess Shale site in British Columbia, Canada, is now high up in the Rocky Mountains, but was once the floor of a shallow sea. Millions of years ago, an underwater mudslide buried a wide variety of sea creatures and turned them into an amazing collection of marine fossils.

The Ottoia prolifica *was a worm-like creature that lived in a U-shaped tunnel in the seabed. Around 1,500 fossils of the creature have been found in the Burgess Shale.*

The *Opabinia* looks like a miniature vacuum cleaner. It had five eyes and a long tube-like nose that scientists think may have been used to suck up tiny worms. The *Amiskwia* is another mysterious sea dweller. It looks like a flat worm with fins on either side of its body and two **tentacles** on the front. It was like a cross between a slug and an arrow worm. The *Wiwaxia* is a bit like an upside-down scrub brush. It had two rows of spines down its back and its oval body was flat and covered with hard plates.

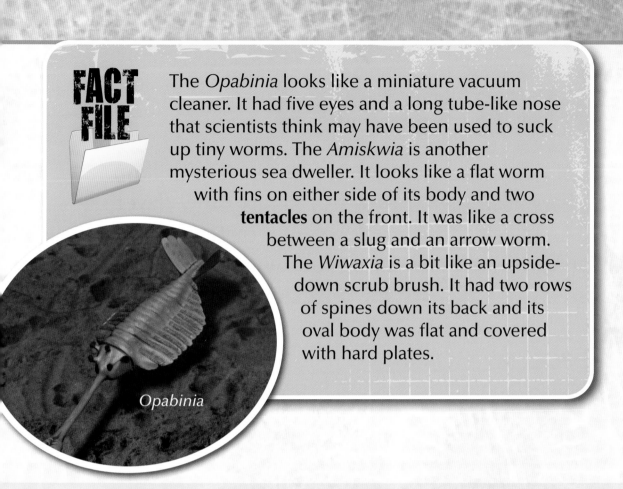

Opabinia

The Burgess Shale is a snapshot of life half a billion years ago. Some of the fossilized creatures found are similar to modern marine animals. Other creatures are so strange looking that paleontologists can find no modern creature that they resemble.

How would a cast mold of an ocean animal be created?

UNDER THE SEA

Fish first appeared on Earth about 530 million years ago. The earliest fish fossils show that they had no jaws so they couldn't bite. Instead they used muscles to suck prey into their mouths. Some of these jawless fish are the ancestors of lamprey eels.

ARE YOU MY MOMMY?

Several million years later, fish had developed jaws and teeth and some grew to enormous sizes, some as long as 21 feet (7 m)! Other fish fossils show that some air-breathing fish were spending more time on land. They were growing primitive lungs and bony fins called "lobe-fins." These became the ancestors of all land creatures, including humans.

NOTEWORTHY NAMES

Elizabeth Philpot was an Englishwoman who lived along the south coast of England in Dorset. She was one of the first fossilists and was known for her amazing collection of fish fossils.

These fossilized teeth once belonged to a megalodon, an extinct species of shark.

FROM FINS TO LIMBS

On Ellesmere Island in Canada's Arctic, paleontologists discovered a fossil of the *Tiktaalik* fish. The *Tiktaalik's* fins show a simple wrist and even the beginnings of fingers. It is important because it appears to show the **transition** from fish to land dweller. It also shows how Earth's land is moving as this island was once a warm, wet forest.

This drawing shows how scientists believe the Tiktaalik *fish may have looked.*

SUPERSIZE ME

The megalodon was an ancient shark of terrifying size. It was over 50 feet (15 m) in length. When it opened its mouth wide, it was so large that a car could have driven into it. It was powerful, but clumsy. With a change to its hunting grounds, it became extinct.

This drawing gives you an idea of the size of the megalodon when compared to a human.

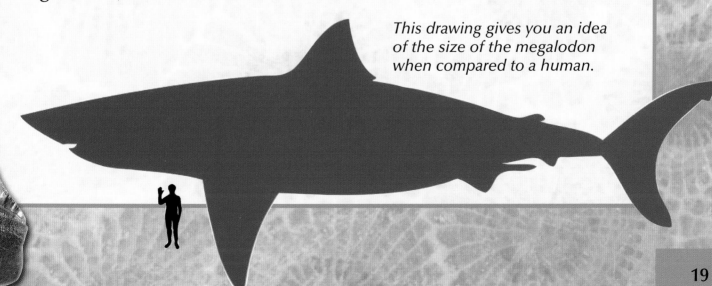

SLITHER AND CRAWL

Paleoherpetologists study the fossils of amphibians (frogs and toads), and reptiles (snakes and crocodiles). The fossil record for amphibians starts about 370 million years ago. Reptiles are younger, they are only about 200 million years old.

CRAWLING ALONG

Amphibians evolved from lobe-finned fish. The earliest amphibian fossil showed the hip, shoulder, leg bones, and jaw of a land-living creature called an *Elginerpeton*. Other fossil amphibians include a small snake-like animal and a creature with a triangular skull and flat tail. Most of these prehistoric amphibians became extinct.

The oldest fossil frogs show that they had a short tail and could swim but not hop.

THEY'RE EVERYWHERE!

While the most famous reptiles, the dinosaurs, did not survive extinction, many other reptile groups did. Reptiles can be found today on every continent except Antarctica and many have not changed much over millions of years.

TIP-TOE THROUGH HISTORY

The oldest reptile fossil is a trace fossil. Footprints found in Nova Scotia, Canada, show reptilian toes and the imprint of scales. This fossil is nearly 315 million years old and belongs to the lizard-like creature *Hylonomus*.

Hylonomus had sharp teeth to catch and eat insects.

GIANT TURTLES

The fossil of the *Archelon* turtle showed that the animal was the size of a small car. Ancient turtles only had a shell on their underside. Strong ribs covered the tops of their bodies. Fossils also show they had teeth instead of beaks like modern turtles. *Archelon* used their teeth to bite into squid, their favorite meal. The beaks of modern turtles are ideal for ripping sea grass and scraping algae.

The Archelon *turtle was the largest sea turtle on Earth.*

? How are ancient turtles different from modern ones?

GIANT MAMMALS

The fossils of mammals show an explosion of evolution **after the extinction of the dinosaurs. Without these huge reptile predators, surviving mammals took up new positions at the top of the food chain.**

A WHALE OF A TALE

Fossils from early mammals showed that these animals were giant-sized. A monster-sized whale, the *Livyatan melvillei*, could grow up to almost 59 feet (18 m) in length, but even scarier were the size of its teeth. Fossil teeth have been found that were more than 14 inches (36 centimeters) long!

Fossilized teeth from the Livyatan melvillei *last longer than fossilized bones because tooth* **enamel** *is one of the hardest substances in a creature's body.*

HOW BIG?

The largest rodent was about the size of a hippopotamus. It grew to be 10 feet (3 m) long and 5 feet (1.5 m) tall! This was no match for the largest land-mammal of all time, however. A type of hornless rhinoceros called the *Indricotherium* grew to be 18 feet (5.5 m) tall!

The *Indricotherium* *towered over other creatures.*

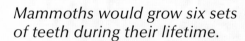

SHRINKING DOWN TO SIZE

The fossil record shows that after mammals evolved to these gigantic sizes, they became smaller again over time. Scientists believe that changes in climate and food sources might be the reason. They can track these changes in mammals by examining fossilized teeth.

Mammoths would grow six sets of teeth during their lifetime.

FACT FILE Whales are mammals, not fish. Fossils show that whales did not evolve from prehistoric fish, but instead evolved from wolf-like animals called Mesonychids that lived on land. As these meat-eating "wolves on hooves" evolved, their legs disappeared and they grew tails to move through water.

FEATHERS AND FLIGHT

Compared to other animal fossils, the fossil record for birds is small. The bones of birds are light and hollow and easily break down. It is not often that they survive the fossilization process.

A paleontologist studies rare bird fossils.

GROUNDED!

The oldest bird fossil is 160 million years old, and was found in Lianoning, China. The *Aurornis* is an extinct bird that was about the size of a pheasant. It had only a few **downy** feathers, so scientists do not believe it could fly. It also had clawed hands, a long tail, and a toothed jaw.

READY TO FLY

Paleontologists began to see changes in the bird fossils over time. Ancient birds lost their bony tails and grew tail feathers instead. They also developed strong shoulders for powerful flight. Ancestors of ostriches, ducks, loons, and gulls have been found in fossils 65 million years old.

GLIDING REPTILES

Many paleontologists believe birds evolved from dinosaurs. Several early bird fossils show this slow transition as **theropod** dinosaurs grew feathers and developed wings and beaks. One ancient fossil that paleontologists believe is the ancestor of crows and turkeys shows a bird with large leg feathers. Scientists believe these feathers may have helped the creature fly or glide.

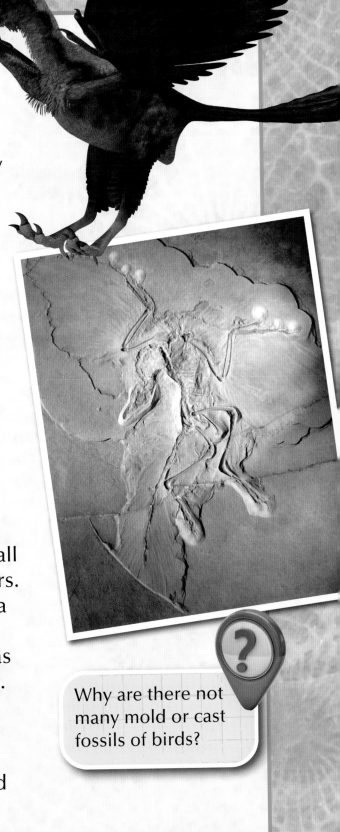

The Archaeopteryx *is believed to be the link between feathered dinosaurs and modern birds.*

WHERE DO THEY BELONG?

The line between bird-like dinosaur and dinosaur-like bird is blurry. Not all birds fly. Some dinosaurs had feathers. So how do scientists know whether a fossil is a bird or a dinosaur? Paleontologists look at whether is has more bird or dinosaur **characteristics**. For instance, the *Archaeopteryx* is considered one of the earliest bird fossils. Like birds it had feathers, wings, and strong legs but it also had teeth and a bony tail like reptiles.

Why are there not many mold or cast fossils of birds?

PAST AND PRESENT

The study of animal fossils is an exciting field. Scientists are looking to the past to figure out how animals adapted to climate change and how we might learn from their successes and failures. There are new discoveries made all the time.

HOW DID IT GET THERE?

A fossil found in Madagascar has presented scientists with a mystery. The fossil is of a giant frog called *Beelzebufo*. Its closest relatives are in South America, and scientists are trying to explain how these two landmasses might have been connected in ancient times.

Beelzebufo *frog*

DNA FROM EGGS

Scientists have developed a way to take DNA from fossilized eggshells of extinct birds. Thanks to fossilized eggs, scientists now have the DNA from one of the heaviest birds that ever lived, the elephant bird called *Aepyornis*.

An elephant bird's egg is 160 times the size of a chicken egg.

LIVING FOSSILS

Living fossils are organisms that have stayed almost unchanged over millions of years. They often survived several mass extinctions and may have strange habits or features that give scientists a hint at life long ago.

tuatara

TUATARA

The tuatara looks like a lizard but is only a distant relative of them. It looks almost the same as its fossil ancestors from 200 million years ago.

nautilus

NAUTILUS

The nautilus is a strange sea creature that has a very unique shell that is a nearly perfect spiral. Fossil hunters have found fossil nautilus shells 500 million years old.

purple frog

PURPLE FROG

The purple frog is a strange creature that is fat with stubby legs and a pointed **snout**. If you hear it cry, it sounds like a chicken. It has been around for 100 million years.

FUN WITH FOSSILS

This activity will help you make your own animal fossil.
You will need:

clay or plasticine

water

plaster powder

plastic bowl

bucket

wooden skewer or
match stick

wooden spoon

brown paint and paint brush

1. Use the clay to make a 3D model of an animal, egg, or footprint. When it is finished, place it in the plastic bowl.

2. Mix the plaster in the bucket with the amount of water suggested on the package. Stir with a wooden spoon.

3. Pour the plaster mix over the clay model in the bowl. Make sure the clay doesn't float.

4. Wait a couple of days for the plaster to dry completely.

5. Tip the plaster out of the bowl. Use a match stick or bamboo skewer to dig out all the clay from the plaster mold.

6. If you want your fossil to look realistic, paint it brown.

Make sure your model will fit at the bottom of your plastic bowl.

GLOSSARY

acidic Containing chemicals that dissolve metals

adapt To change to fit a new environment

ancestors Organisms that came before

asphalt A thick, dark, sticky liquid

bacteria One-celled organisms

casts 3D models of mold fossils created by hardened minerals

characteristics Features that make something different from something else

crevasse A deep, open crack in a glacier

decomposed Describing something decayed or rotting away

diversity A great variety

downy Covered with fine, soft hair or feathers

enamel The hard, white coating on teeth

evolution The slow development from one thing to another

evolved Changed and developed slowly over time

exterior The outside of something

extinct Describing a species that no longer exists

glaciers Slow-moving rivers of ice

organism A living animal or plant

parasites Organisms that live in and feed off of other organisms

preserved Kept from rotting away

sediment Fine dirt that settles to the bottom of a lake or ocean

snout The nose and mouth of an animal

tentacles Long, flexible growths around the mouths of certain animals

theropod A meat-eating dinosaur that walked on two legs

transition Changing from one thing to another

LEARNING MORE

FURTHER READING:

Hyde, Natalie. *What are Fossils?* Crabtree Publishing, 2012.

Parker, Steve. *Fossil Hunting: An Expert Guide to Finding and Identifying Fossils and Creating a Collection.* Anness Publishing, 2009.

Taylor, Paul. *Eyewitness Fossil.* Dorling Kindersley Ltd., 2004.

Thomson, Sarah. *Ancient Animals: Terror Bird.* Charlesbridge Publishing, 2013.

WEBSITES:

The latest discoveries on Science News for Kids:

www.sciencenewsforkids.org/2012/11/for-more-than-a-century-the-fossilized-skull-of-an-ancient-fish-was-misidentified-as-a-primate/

Science Kids website with fun fossil facts for kids:

www.sciencekids.co.nz/sciencefacts/earth/fossils.html

Fossil information fun for kids of all ages:

www.fossilsforkids.com

Fossil Facts part of Dialogue for Kids by Idaho Public Television:

www.wacona.com/promote/fossils/animal.htm

INDEX

air-breathing fish, 18, 19
amber fossils, 8–9
ammonite shells, 6
amphibians, 20
ancient Greeks, 4

bacteria, 5, 7, 8, 11
birds, 9, 24–25, 26
blue-green algae, 5
bones, 4, 6, 11, 15, 18, 20, 22, 24
Buckland, Reverend William, 15
Burgess Shale, 16, 17

casts, 6
connected landmasses, 26
coprolites, 15
Cuvier, Georges, 5

decomposing, 6, 7, 8
dinosaurs 15, 20, 22, 25
DNA, 13, 26

earliest known fossils, 5
early humans, 13, 18
eggs, 9, 15, 26
evolution, 9, 19, 20, 22, 23, 25
extinction, 5, 20, 22, 27

feathers, 8, 24, 25
fish fossils, 15, 18, 19, 20
footprints, 14, 21
fossil formation, 6
fossilists, 18
frogs, 20, 26, 27
frozen fossils, 7, 12–13
fur, 7, 12

glaciers, 7, 12

hair, 7, 8, 12

imprints, 4, 21
index fossils, 7
insects, 8, 9, 10, 21

jaws, 18, 20, 24

La Brea Tar Pits, 10
living fossils, 27
lizards, 9, 21

make your own fossil, 28–29
mammals, 4, 5, 10, 11, 12, 13, 22–23
mastodons, 5, 12
megalodon, 18, 19
mineralized fossils, 6, 16
mold fossils, 6, 16
monster myths, 4

nautilus, 27
nests, 14, 15

paleoherpetologists, 20
paleontologists, 5, 15, 25
peat bogs, 7, 11
Philpot, Elizabeth, 17
plants, 5, 8–9, 10
poop, 14, 15
preserved remains, 4, 7, 8–9

reading fossil history, 7
reptiles, 6, 9, 20–21, 25
rhinoceroses, 4, 23

scorpion, 8
sea life, 6, 7, 16–19, 21, 22, 23, 27

tar pits, 7, 10
teeth, 6, 18, 22, 23, 24, 25
trace fossils, 14–15, 21
tree resin, 8–9
trilobites, 7
tuatara, 27
turtles, 15, 21

whales, 22, 23
woolly mammoths, 4, 5, 10, 12, 13, 23